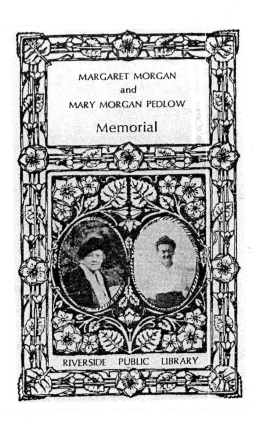

MARGARET MORGAN
and
MARY MORGAN PEDLOW

Memorial

RIVERSIDE PUBLIC LIBRARY

HEINEMANN
STATE STUDIES

California
History

Mir Tamim Ansary

Heinemann Library
Chicago, Illinois

© 2003 Heinemann Library
a division of Reed Elsevier Inc.
Chicago, Illinois

Customer Service 888-454-2279

Visit our website at www.heinemannlibrary.com

Designed by Heinemann Library
Page layout by Depke Design
Printed and bound in the United States by
Lake Book Manufacturing, Inc.

07 06 05 04 03
10 9 8 7 6 5 4 3 2 1

**Library of Congress
Cataloging-in-Publication Data**
Ansary, Mir Tamim.
   California history / by Mir Tamim Ansary.
     p. cm. -- (Heinemann state studies)
   Includes bibliographical references (p.) and
index.
   Contents: Early California -- Becoming the Gold-
en State -- California enters the modern era -- Pros-
perity, depression, and world war -- Living in a
Modern World -- Timeline.
     ISBN 1-40340-340-6 -- ISBN 1-40340-557-3
(pbk.)
   1. California--History--Juvenile literature.
[1.California--History.]   I. Title. II. Series.
   F861.3.A46 2002
   979.4--dc21

2002010888

Acknowledgments
The author and publishers are grateful to the
following for permission to reproduce copyright
material:

Cover photographs by (top, L-R) The Society
of California Pioneers, Bettmann/Corbis,
Bettmann/Corbis, The Bancroft Library/University
of California, Berkeley, (main) Bob Krist/Corbis

Title page (L-R) The Granger Collection, Franklin D.
Roosevelt Library, The Granger Collection; contents
page (L-R) The Granger Collection, Bettmann/
Corbis; pp. 4, 5, 8T, 15, 16, 23, 25, 27B, 29, 32,
37 The Granger Collection; pp. 6, 22, 27T, 33, 35,
39 Bettmann/Corbis; pp. 7, 13, 18, 28, 44
maps.com/Heinemann Library; p. 8B Richard
Cummins/Corbis; pp. 10, 19, 21 The Bancroft
Library/University of California, Berkeley; p. 12
Brown Brothers; p. 14T The Society of California
Pioneers; p. 14B Stock Montage, Inc.; p. 20
Huntington Library; pp. 24, 36 Franklin D.
Roosevelt Library; p. 30 Lloyd Cluff/Corbis; p. 31
Corbis; p. 34 Library of Congress; p. 38 U.S. Air
Force/AP Wide World Photos; p. 40 Ron Edmonds/
AP Wide World Photos; p. 41 Ralph Morse/
TimePix; p. 42 David Butow/Corbis SABA; p. 43 Bill
Ross/Corbis

Photo research by Kathy Creech

Special thanks to Lucinda Surber for her curriculum
guidance.

Every effort has been made to contact copyright
holders of any material reproduced in this book.
Any omissions will be rectified in subsequent
printings if notice is given to the publisher.

Some words are shown in bold, **like this.**
You can find out what they mean by looking
in the glossary.

Contents

Early California 4

Becoming the Golden State 16

California Enters the Modern Era 24

Depression and World War 34

Living in the Modern World 38

Map of California 44

Timeline 45

Glossary 46

More Books to Read 47

Index 48

About the Author 48

Early California

For many centuries, nature isolated California from the rest of the world. Mountains, deserts, and the world's largest ocean surround the land. Therefore, people wandered in very slowly, over thousands of years. Most walked in from the north or east, but some may have come by boat from Asia or islands in the Pacific Ocean.

By 2000 B.C.E., small groups of people lived in every part of California. Only the few people who lived near the Colorado River, in the south, did any farming. The rest lived on food they gathered or hunted, and since the land was so plentiful, they survived without much struggle.

When explorers first found California, it was so isolated by landforms and water that many people believed it was an island. The present-day Colorado River is labeled on this early map as the Rio del Norte, *or* North River.

They had only simple weapons and rarely made war. By 1512, about 300,000 people lived in what is now California.

EXPLORERS ARRIVE (1512)

That year, Europeans came to the North American continent. They first settled on the islands Hispaniola, Jamaica, and Trinidad in the Caribbean Sea. The Spaniard Hernán Cortés landed on the east coast of Mexico with a group of soldiers. He conquered the native peoples in that area and made it the center of a new Spanish empire.

In 1533, Francisco de Ulloa landed on the large **peninsula** now known as Baja California. *Baja* means "lower." He also sailed far enough north to be sure that Baja California was not an island, as many explorers thought. In 1542, a sea captain named Juan Rodríguez Cabrillo sailed into San Diego Bay. From that year on, many European explorers visited California.

Hernán Cortés sent men to explore the North American continent, hoping to find cities of gold.

One of these explorers was the English sea captain Francis Drake. He stopped in California on his way around the world. The Spanish considered Drake a pirate because he kept robbing their ships. But Queen Elizabeth I of England thought him to be her loyal servant, because England and Spain were enemies at the time. She made Drake a knight in reward for serving his duty. Sir Francis Drake in turn claimed California for her.

The Miwok believed Sir Francis Drake and his men were sea gods, because the explorers arrived by ship. The Miwok crowned Drake as their king.

NAMING THE LAND

After Drake sailed away, most of the early explorers of the area were Spaniards. Some believe they named the land *California* after a popular adventure story of the time. In that story, a knight found a wonderful island called *Califia,* halfway between heaven and earth.

MISSIONS (1769-1834)

In 1769, Gaspar de Portola started the next stage of California history. Spain owned rich colonies in Asia, so it was interested in California mainly as a place for ships

Explorers played an important role in mapping out the area we know as California today.

California Explorers (1539–1769)

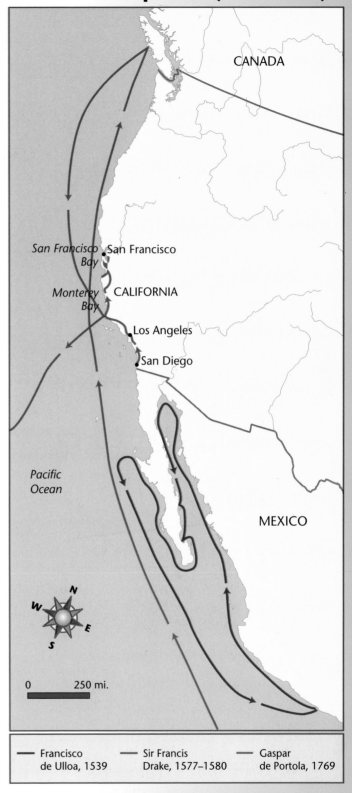

Francisco de Ulloa, 1539 — Sir Francis Drake, 1577–1580 — Gaspar de Portola, 1769

to stop on their way to and from Asia. Portola came to California with a group that included **Catholic** priest Junípero Serra. Juan Crespí, another Spanish explorer, joined Portola, and they went to find Monterey Bay, which an earlier explorer had seen from far away.

Portola sailed north and found San Francisco Bay. Father Serra, however, stopped in San Diego. Father Serra was a **missionary** and wanted to lead Native Americans to follow **Christianity** and join the **Catholic Church.**

In San Diego, Serra and his followers built a **mission,** a small town based around a church. Missionaries offered gifts to people for coming to learn about Christianity. However, those who came to the mission were not allowed to leave—they became slaves.

Father Serra and his followers built a total of 21 missions along the California coast, from San Diego to Sonoma. The sites for each of the missions were carefully selected by the missionaries. The sites had to have good supplies of water and fertile soils for growing crops. Most

In 1769, Father Junípero Serra founded the first Spanish mission in California, at San Diego.

importantly, the **missions** had to be located near large populations of native peoples in order to fully develop. A highway called *El Camino Real*, or "The Royal Road," connected them. Today, that old route is called Highway 101, but many California coastal cities have a major street called El Camino Real.

Many missions grew quite wealthy, thanks to the hard work of Native Americans. They farmed the land, made wine, and tended cattle. All of the missions had buildings for shops for **blacksmithing, tanning,** candle making, basket weaving, leather working, and furniture making.

Mission Architecture

The Spanish **missionaries** in California developed a building style all their own. Typical missions were made of **adobe,** a type of clay. They had thick, strong walls to stand up to California's earthquakes. The buildings had open courtyards, long rows of columns, arched doorways, and many hallways. The roofs were covered with red

tiles, which were made of baked clay that would not catch fire. This picture is of Mission Santa Ines, established in 1804, and located in Santa Barbara County.

The missions played a large part in turning native peoples from a hunter-gatherer society toward an agricultural one. On large areas of land they grew grains and fruits, including palms, olives, grapes, figs, oranges, and pomegranates. They had also large herds of cattle and horses and huge flocks of sheep.

PRESIDIOS AND PUEBLOS

Spain sent soldiers to protect the priests, and four **forts** called *presidios* were built. The purpose of the *presidios* was to protect Spanish towns, ranches, mining camps, and towns of friendly Indians, and to open up new territories for the Spanish to settle. The *presidio* also was a place where friendly natives came to settle, receive protection against their enemies, and get gifts of clothing, food, and other items. These *presidios* were located in San Diego, San Francisco, Monterey, and Santa Barbara.

It was a big problem, however, to get enough food for the soldiers at the *presidios*. Government officials tried to fix this problem by founding **pueblos** near the missions in northern and southern California.

California Cowboys

The Native Americans and Mexicans who did the work on *ranchos* were called *vaqueros*, which is a Spanish word meaning "cowboys." They rode horses, wore **chaps,** and roped cattle, just like cowboys in Texas and elsewhere. The first **rodeos** were held in California, and the practice of branding cattle started there, too. Cows **grazed** freely and were then rounded up. Brands helped ranchers know which cows belonged to whom.

To attract settlers to the new towns, the government provided free land, livestock, farming equipment, and **annual** funding for clothing and other supplies. Also, new settlers did not have to pay any taxes for five years. In return, the settlers were required to sell their **surplus** agricultural products to the *presidios*.

The first city to be established from a *pueblo* was San Jose, founded in 1777. It was followed in 1781 by El Pueblo de Nuestra Señora la Reina de los Angeles del Río de Porciúncula, now known simply as Los Angeles.

Mariano G. Vallejo, shown here with family members, was one of eight Californios *to serve in California's* **constitutional convention.** *He was a* ranchero *and also served in the first California state senate.*

A MEXICAN PROVINCE (1821–1848)

In 1821, Mexico gained its independence from Spain. California became a **province** in the new nation of Mexico. It was ruled by governors from Mexico City. Mexican settlers in California were known as *Californios.*

The new Mexican republic wanted to **secularize** the **missions,** taking control of the property from the Franciscan **missionaries.** Although most Mexicans were **Catholic,** they disliked the power and wealth of the **Catholic Church.** After the missions were seized, the lands were to be divided among the Native Americans living there. Instead, the land went to *Californio* families such

A True Mountain Man

Although James Beckwourth (1798–1867?) was born a slave, his white father eventually declared his son a "free Negro" and brought him out west. As a young man, Beckwourth lived among the Crow Indians, marrying a number of Crow women. Later, he guided gold hunters through the mountains to California, blazing a new trail through the Sierra Nevada Mountains. This trail was later named Beckwourth Pass, and is still in use today by Pacific Railroad and the U.S. Interstate Highway System. Beckwourth also served as guide and **interpreter** for U.S. troops during the Cheyenne War of 1864.

as the Picos, Alvarados, Vallejos, and Castros, who became rich and powerful. Between 1822 and 1846, more than 800 California **land grants** were made to individuals by the Mexican government. As a result, *ranchos,* huge estates on large areas of land, were established. The Pico *rancho,* for example, covered over 500,000 acres—almost as much land as is in the whole state of Rhode Island.

LIFE OF A CALIFORNIO

The *Californios* raised horses and cattle on their *ranchos.* They ate the beef from the cattle and sold the hides, from which leather could be made. Cowhides, called "California bank notes," were even used as money in California during the 1830s and 1840s. The *rancho* owners, or *rancheros,* sold tallow, too. Tallow is used to make soap, candles, and other goods.

NEW SETTLERS

Meanwhile, Americans were entering California too. A trapper named Jedediah Smith led the way. He entered California in 1826, becoming the first American to enter California from the east. The *Californios* threw him out, but he kept coming back. He opened the coastal route from California to **Fort** Vancouver on the Columbia River. Smith was killed by Commanche Indians in 1831.

DEMAND FOR LAND

In 1844, a new kind of adventurer arrived. John C. Frémont said he was in California to **survey** land, but his men were all soldiers in the U.S. Army. Secretly, he was working for Thomas Hart Benton, a U.S. senator. Frémont was married to Benton's daughter. Senator Benton believed the Mexicans were going to lose control of California, and he feared that the British would then move in, so he sent his son-in-law to take control of California if he had a chance.

However, U.S. President James Polk did not trust Senator Benton or Frémont. He sent his own **agent,** John Slidell, to California. Slidell had orders to discuss buying from Mexico the land that is now California and New Mexico.

When the Mexican government refused to speak to Slidell, U.S. Army troops under the command of General Zachary Taylor advanced to the Rio Grande River in Texas. The United States declared war on Mexico on May 13, 1846.

John C. Frémont

THE MEXICAN-AMERICAN WAR (1846–1848)

There were three main issues that drove the United States to declare war on Mexico. The first issue was the **annexation** of Texas on December 29, 1845. Although Texas was an independent republic, Mexico still claimed the land as its own. Mexico was upset that Texas was to become a U.S. state, and felt that, if challenged, the Mexican army would be able to defeat U.S. soldiers and get the land back.

Mexican-American War Land Claims

Map labels:
- UNITED STATES
- Fort Leavenworth
- Sutter's Fort
- San Francisco
- Monterey
- Bent's Fort
- Colorado River
- Los Angeles
- San Pascual
- Gila River
- San Diego
- Texas boundary as claimed by Texas
- Texas boundary as claimed by Mexico
- Rio Grande
- Nueces River
- PACIFIC OCEAN
- Guadalupe-Hidalgo Treaty Boundary Line
- Corpus Christi
- Monterrey
- Gulf of Mexico
- MEXICO
- Mazatlán
- Tampico
- N W E S
- 0 250 mi
- Mexico City

Territory of Mexico lost to the United States

The next issue was the Mexican government refused to pay the money they owed to U.S. citizens who had been injured or had property damaged by the frequent Mexican battles at that time. Finally, the United States wanted to gain the land that is now California, which was currently a Mexican **province.** The United States was afraid that the weakness of the Mexican government might cause California to fall under British or French rule.

This map outlines the territory that both the United States and Mexico felt they could claim. After the Mexican-American War, the land became part of the United States.

The current California state flag is very similar to this one, which was flown during the "Bear Flag Revolt."

BEAR FLAG REVOLT

Meanwhile, on June 11, 1846, about 30 of Frémont's friends stormed the home of Mariano Vallejo, the Mexican governor of northern California, taking him prisoner. The rebels did not want California to be under Mexican rule any longer. By capturing Vallejo, they were one step closer to their goal. They raised a flag with a picture of a grizzly bear on it and declared the beginning of the "California Republic." This event became known as the Bear Flag **Revolt.**

The new republic only lasted about a month, however. The rebels were not aware that the United States was already at war with Mexico. On July 7, 1846, U.S. troops led by **Commodore** John Sloat arrived. The town of Monterey surrendered to Sloat and his troops.

In 1846, a group of angry men arrested the Mexican governor and declared California an independent republic.

CLAIMING CALIFORNIA

In the next few months, the United States completed its **conquest** of California. Commodore Robert Stockton replaced Sloat. He organized the army, and marched through northern California, flying the American flag. He took control of Los Angeles, and continued to walk the land, claiming it for the United States. There was no opposition from California residents. Mexican rule had left them with no supplies and little desire to fight.

In the south, General Stephen Kearny marched in from Nevada. However, an army of *Californios* trapped his forces at San Pascual. The battle that followed was the largest ever fought in California—22 soldiers died. Kearny sent word for Stockton to come help. Stockton came and helped Kearny recapture nearby Los Angeles.

Eleven days later, on February 2, 1848, Mexico and the United States signed a peace treaty at Guadalupe-Hidalgo. Mexico received $15 million for what is now California, Texas, Arizona, New Mexico, Nevada, and Utah, as well as parts of Colorado and Wyoming.

The Battle of San Pascual, on December 6, 1846, was a defeat for the U.S. Army. This was due to General Kearny's not knowing of the fighting abilities of the Californios.

Becoming the Golden State

The year 1848 marked a great turning point in California history. With the end of the Mexican-American War, California no longer was under Mexican control. In this same year, gold was discovered at a place called Sutter's Mill.

Sutter's Mill belonged to Johann Augustus Sutter, a Swiss **immigrant.** Sutter owned 50,000 acres near the Sierra Nevada Mountains. He built a **fort** there called New Helvetia. Nearly everyone who came to California arrived at Sutter's Fort. Sutter was well-known for being friendly and helpful to everyone he met, providing supplies to those who needed them after a long journey.

Most assume Johann Sutter, owner of Sutter's Fort (below), was a rich man, but he actually left California with no money.

On January 24, 1848, one of Sutter's workers found flecks of gold in the stream below the mill. Sutter tried to hide the discovery, but he could not keep it from newsman Sam Brannan. Brannan had just started California's first newspaper. He also owned a store at New Helvetia. When Brannan learned the great secret, he quietly stocked his store with everything a miner might need. Then he rode through San Francisco with a bag of gold dust, shouting "Gold!"

THE GOLD RUSH (1848–1859)

Brannan's news swept the country and the world. People headed for California in any way they could. Some crossed the Great Plains in big wagons called prairie schooners. This hard journey took at least 100 days. Others came by sea, sailing around South America, often through stormy waters. This journey took at least six months. Some sailed only to Panama in Central America. Then they walked north across the isthmus, the thin strip of land connecting North and South America. They had to push through thick jungle, and many of them died of tropical diseases along the way. Once they reached the Pacific coast of Central America, they had to wait for weeks or even months for a ship to take them up to California.

Dame Shirley

One of the best eyewitness accounts of the gold rush is a set of letters written by Dame Shirley, the **pen name** of Louise Amelia Knapp Smith Clappe. Dame Shirley told the stories of the hard life of mining. She described the harsh conditions that often were forgotten by those in later years who told stories of the "greatness" of the gold rush.

California During the Gold Rush

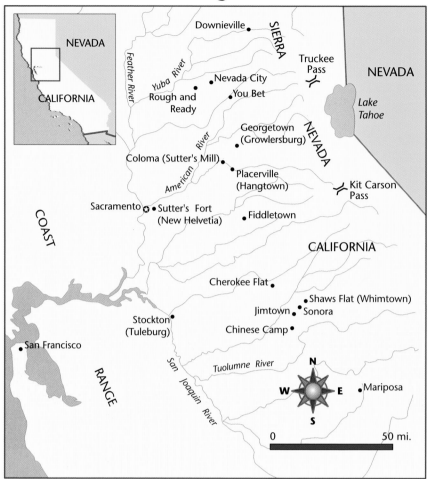

In 1848, a national news radio broadcast declared: "Gold is everywhere you look, sparkling in the sun and glittering in the streams. It lies on the open plain and it glows on the mountains."

All the towns listed on this map were gold rush towns. The names in parentheses were the names of the towns during the gold rush.

But even such a long journey could not stop the gold-hungry "forty-niners," nicknamed for arriving in 1849. As people arrived, gold mining towns sprang up almost overnight. They were rough and lawless places. Most homes were just tents, and there was plenty of drinking and fighting. Yet miners found good friendships in the camps, too. At night, they often sat around campfires, telling stories and singing songs. On Sundays, they took time off to wash and mend their clothes, chop firewood for the week, and cook meals of bread and pork and beans to be eaten during the week.

Miners found millions of dollars worth of gold in the streams of California, yet few got rich. Soon after gold was mined, there was too much money and not enough food and supplies to buy with it. The people who supplied the miners made most of the money. They sold

Many miners separated gold from sand by washing the mixture in a simple rocking box called a cradle. The pieces of gold sank to the bottom of the pan as the sand was washed away.

shovels, food, entertainment, mules, and supplies at high prices. The miners had to pay whatever was asked because this was their only source of supplies. They felt they could afford it since they thought they were going to find so much gold!

CULTURE CLASH

Many mines, especially in the south, were worked by people from other countries who came only for the gold. Chinese, Chileans, Mexicans, Irish, Germans, French, and Turks all sought their fortune in California.

Like American-born miners, foreign miners had no plans for staying in California. Their goal was to get the gold and go home. As gold became less plentiful, however, anger toward foreigners grew. Under pressure, the California legislature passed the Foreign Miners Tax in 1850. This was a $20 per month tax to be paid by every foreign miner.

John Bidwell

John Bidwell came to California from Missouri with the first group to **emigrate** across the country, and went on to play a large role in the state's history. Upon his arrival, he went to work at Sutter's **Fort.** After the Bear Flag **Revolt,** he helped create the Bear Flag Republic's resolution of independence in July 1846.

Bidwell fought in the Mexican-American War, marching to Monterey with Colonel John C. Frémont, and he assisted **Commodore** Robert F. Stockton in the recapture of Los Angeles in 1847. At the end of the war, Bidwell returned to Sutter's Fort and became the first to find gold.

With his newly discovered wealth, Bidwell purchased a 22,000-acre ranch, Rancho Chico, north of Sacramento. There he became the state's leading **agriculturalist** while also serving in the state senate. He was elected to the U.S. House of Representatives in 1864; and in 1892, he was a U.S. presidential candidate for the **Prohibition Party.**

Many foreign miners refused to pay the tax and left the country. Others, like the Chinese, stayed in California, in mining, or in more traditional jobs. Although there were occasional problems, most of these new residents thrived. Almost instantly, the state had the most diverse **ethnic culture** in the world.

SILVER MINING

The gold rush reached its peak in 1852, but by 1859, gold was running low. Silver mining took the place of gold mining. However, expensive equipment is needed to separate silver from rock. Big companies had to be

formed for it to work. In gold rush San Francisco, there were few men ready to form such companies.

The richest silver mine in the area was the Comstock Lode. Although it was in Nevada, its owners lived in

New technologies like "square set" timbering had to be used for silver mining. This was because, unlike gold, the treasure lay deep in the ground.

San Francisco. People made more money from silver than anyone had made from gold. Because of all the money being made, San Francisco became the most populated city in the West. During the silver rush, San Francisco grew from 812 people to 25,000. A new city, Sacramento, formed near the hills where gold was mined.

BECOMING A STATE

Most of the gold rush newcomers were Americans. They wanted California to join the United States, but there was a problem. The United States was struggling with the terrible issue of slavery at this time. Southern states allowed people to own slaves, while northern states—called free states—did not. Some people in the North, called **abolitionists,** wanted to ban slavery completely. California planned to join the **Union** as a free state, but this would mean that there were more free states than slave states represented in **Congress.** If that happened, Congress could then pass laws against slavery. This led Southern politicians to keep California out of the Union.

On January 29, 1850, Missouri Senator Henry Clay presented the Compromise of 1850 to Congress. It stated that California would join as a free state, but it also contained the Fugitive Slave Act. This Act allowed for the capture of slaves who had run away from their owners in the South. The Compromise was debated by members of Congress for eight months before it was finally accepted.

Senator Henry Clay, known as the "Great Compromiser," came out of retirement to help Congress find a solution to the problem of whether to allow California to join the Union.

Meanwhile, 48 important Californians gathered to draft a state constitution. Two of the issues addressed in the meetings were whether women could own land and where the eastern border of California should be. The delegates voted for women to be allowed to own land, which made California the first state to grant this privilege. The most difficult decision was where the eastern border of the state should be. It was drawn at the eastern slope of the Sierra Nevada, where it still stands today.

On October 29, 1850, San Franciscans gathered to celebrate California's newly established statehood.

On September 9, 1850, California became the 31st state, with San Jose as the first state capital. Lack of housing and poor climate forced the state capital to move from San Jose to Vallejo in 1852, and then to Benicia in 1853. Sacramento became the permanent location of the state capital on February 25, 1854.

California Enters the Modern Era

The Civil War, changes in transportation, and advances in communication connected the new state of California with the rest of the nation and the world.

CIVIL WAR (1861–1865)

During the Civil War, most Californians sided with the North. Only 15,000 Californians joined the army. Of these, few went east where the battles took place. Even so, California did play a large part in the war. One reason the North won was because it had more factories. It could make more cannons, guns, and other supplies. $785 million from California's gold was used to build factories and provide supplies.

California gold helped pay for Northern victories in Civil War battles like this one at Gettysburg, Pennsylvania.

TRANSCONTINENTAL RAILROAD (1863–1869)

For California, the key event of this period occurred in 1862. **Congress** passed a law calling for a railroad across the continent to connect the states. At the time, people believed a railroad could never be built over the Sierra Nevada Mountains. One bright engineer, Theodore Judah, disagreed.

Judah signed up four San Francisco merchants as partners. Leland Stanford, Collis Huntington, Charles Crocker, and Mark Hopkins came to be known as the Big Four. Together, these men founded the Central Pacific Railroad Company.

Chinese Workers on the Railroad

The Central Pacific hired about 15,000 Chinese men to help build the railroad. Chinese men who had come for the gold rush were eager to find jobs, and they were willing to work for very little money. These workers chipped tunnels through solid rock in the Sierra Nevada Mountains. One such tunnel was a mile long. Sometimes they worked in baskets hanging down the faces of cliffs. From there, they chipped out the rock by hand. Many of these workers were injured or killed by their dangerous work.

Communication Tools

Overland Mail Service

In 1858, the U.S. government hired the Southern Overland Mail Company to deliver mail to the Pacific coast. The company operated a 25-day, semi-weekly stagecoach run along a route from St. Louis, Missouri, through El Paso, Texas, and Tucson, New Mexico Territory, to San Francisco, California.

With the outbreak of the Civil War in 1861, the southern route was dropped, and the government contract was awarded to the Central Overland California and Pikes Peak Express. This company ran through Salt Lake City, Utah. The company went out of business after the building of the **transcontinental** railroad in 1869.

Western Union Telegraph Company

The Western Union Telegraph Company was created in 1851 to provide **telegraphic** communications services in the United States. Originally known as the New York and Mississippi Valley Printing Telegraph Company, Western Union built the nation's first transcontinental telegraph line in 1861. Telegraph lines soon connected cities throughout the eastern United States, allowing people to send messages coast to coast.

At the same time, another railroad company, called the Union Pacific, formed in the East. The government gave both companies money and land to lay tracks across the continent. The Central Pacific was to start in Sacramento, California, and work eastward. The Union Pacific was to start in Omaha, Nebraska, and work westward.

The building of the railroad began in 1863. In 1869, the tracks from the east and the west met in Promontory, Utah. The last spike was driven into the ground on May 10th in a great ceremony. The trip from New York to Sacramento, which used to take four to six months, now took just seven days.

The Pony Express

In 1863, the fastest way to send a letter across the country was by Pony Express. This company had a series of stations between St. Joseph, Missouri, and San Francisco, California. Riders could get fresh horses every fifteen miles, and a fresh rider took over every few stations. Thus, a letter traveled as fast as a horse moving nonstop at top speed. It went from Missouri to California in about eleven days. The Pony Express went out of business soon after the transcontinental railroad was built, because a train could take a letter coast to coast in just eight days.

Although the railroad created many new opportunities, all of the people who had built the railroad were now out of work, including thousands of Chinese workers. As the poorest people, the Chinese were often willing to work for very low wages. White workers felt that the Chinese were taking their jobs, so anti-Chinese **riots** broke out. In 1882, the Chinese Exclusion Act was passed into law, banning Chinese people from entering the United States.

*Denis Kearney, pictured in this 1878 cartoon, encouraged the anti-Chinese riots and demanded that Chinese **immigrants** be thrown out of the United States. He gave speeches that ended with "The Chinese must go!"*

Transportation and Mail Routes to California

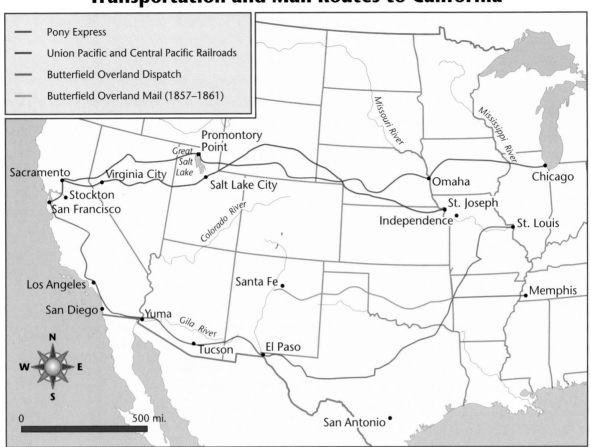

Legend:
- Pony Express
- Union Pacific and Central Pacific Railroads
- Butterfield Overland Dispatch
- Butterfield Overland Mail (1857–1861)

The Pony Express and the **transcontinental** *railroad were quick and efficient ways to move people and mail across the country.*

Although most people struggled during this time, a few kept growing richer. The Big Four and their friends took control of a new railroad company, the Southern Pacific. It built railroads within the state of California. The Southern Pacific was so powerful that it blocked any other railroad from being built. It could charge as much as it wanted for its services.

Farmers were once again raising plenty of crops and cattle. To make money, however, they had to get their wheat, meat, and eggs to market before they spoiled. Competition from the east made this very difficult. Trains started bringing in tons of food and inexpensive goods from the east. Farmers were forced to pay the high prices of using the railroad in order to try to make a living, but California farms could not compete with the east.

Farm owners soon had to look for jobs. Jobs, however, became hard to find.

CROWDING THE STATE

The increase in transportation capabilities opened the door to California for many people. In southern California, **citrus** farming became important. California shipped oranges around the country and oranges became a symbol of the state.

People in the business of selling land took advantage of the state's new image: warm weather, sunshine, and fresh air. They advertised California as "America's Italy." In 1887, more than 200,000 people came to the Los Angeles area. About 100 towns developed within Los Angeles County.

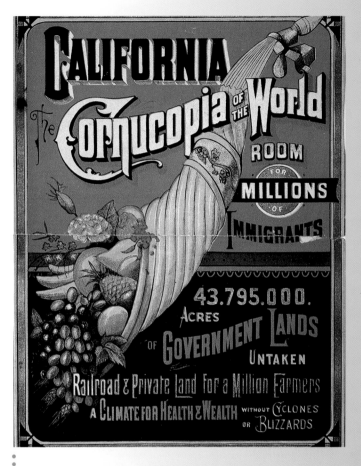

Posters promoting California as a land of good climate and easy money drew many people to southern California.

Henry Huntington, a nephew of Collis Huntington of the Big Four, spotted an opportunity in all this. He built a railroad in Los Angeles County called the Pacific Electric. It was a network of **trolley** lines that connected 46 towns. By 1900, Los Angeles County matched San Francisco County in power and wealth. One thing limited its growth, however: Los Angeles was located in a very dry area and did not have enough water.

The Owens Valley–Los Angeles Aqueduct, finished in 1939, carries water hundreds of miles from northern to southern California.

GETTING WATER

At this point, a city engineer, William Mulholland, came up with a daring plan. He decided to build a canal from the Sierra Nevada Mountains to Los Angeles. The canal he built was called the Owens Valley–Los Angeles **Aqueduct.** It was one of the greatest engineering accomplishments of its time, flowing water by gravity from the Owens Valley to Los Angeles.

DISASTER IN SAN FRANCISCO (1906)

On April 18, 1906, San Francisco was hit with the greatest **catastrophe** in its history. An earthquake measuring 8.3 on the **Richter scale** shook the city for almost a full minute. The earthquake started fires that raged across the city for three days. Over 28,000 buildings burned down and it is estimated that 3,000 people died. When the fires were put out at last, the great city of San Francisco lay in ruins. It took several months to build new structures and clean up the mess the earthquake had left behind.

MOVING FORWARD

The opening of the Panama Canal tied California even closer to the rest of the nation. Completed in 1915, this canal cut across the Isthmus of Panama, the thin strip of land connecting North and South America. Ships could now pass from the Atlantic Ocean to the Pacific Ocean without traveling all the way around South America.

To celebrate the canal, the newly rebuilt city of San Francisco held the

The Panama Canal made traveling by ship much quicker and less dangerous than before.

Panama-Pacific International Exposition in 1915. Over 19 million people visited the fair.

GROWTH OF INDUSTRY

Meanwhile, World War I (1914–1918) had broken out in Europe. The war was good for the economic development of California. Companies in California made ships, airplanes, and other products and materials used in wartime, such as rubber for tires. California entered the 1920s as an **industrial** powerhouse.

The demand for airplanes in World War I started the airplane industry in California.

Another area where California was succeeding was in the entertainment industry. Moviemakers began moving to California around 1905. They came from the East Coast to get away from Thomas Edison, who had invented the movie camera. Edison wanted control over who made movies. By law, no one could make a movie without his permission. Edison had a hard time controlling faraway Los Angeles, however.

D. W. Griffith (behind the camera) was one of the first great movie directors of the 1920s.

Moviemaking did not receive much attention at first, but after the war, it became the state's best-known industry. California's beauty and climate made it an ideal setting for shooting movies. The first movie studio began in 1908, in Los Angeles. *In the Sultan's Power,* directed by Francis Boggs, was the first full-length movie made in California. By 1913, there were 74 movie companies in Los Angeles and Hollywood.

Depression and World War

Despite the success of the movies and war equipment production, business slowed in the 1930s, and the United States entered a **depression.** In fact, this point in U.S. history is called the Great Depression because it was so severe.

Hollywood movies of the 1930s were filled with singing and laughter, but outside the movies, there was not much laughter in the country. Banks were failing, and jobs were vanishing. The Midwest was also in terrible need of some rain. Oklahoma and Arkansas turned into **"dust bowls."** Many crops failed, and small farmers lost their land. Thousands of people headed toward California, believing the stories that said it was where dreams came true. However, many people found only hardship. Most ended up as poor migrant farm workers, moving from field to field, looking for work.

A Rude Welcome

The people who were already in California did not treat newcomers well. No one wanted more competition for the few jobs that existed. The newcomers, who came mostly from Oklahoma and

This mother and her children were so desperate for money to buy food that they sold the tires off their car.

The promise of good weather and farming jobs pushed many dust-bowl farmers west to California. Highway 66 provided a direct route from the dust-bowl states to California.

Arkansas, were given insulting nicknames. They were called "Okies" or "Arkies." In 1939, California went so far as to pass a law stating that no one from the dust bowl states could move there. Police stood guard at the borders, turning away cars as they arrived from certain states. The courts later overruled the law.

WORLD WAR II (1939–1945)

It took another full-scale war to end the Great Depression. When the World War II began in 1939, the United States stayed out of the fighting, but provided weapons and equipment for the **Allies.** California companies once again had goods to produce and jobs to offer. The San Francisco Bay Area became a center for ship building. Airplanes and weapons were produced in southern California.

In 1941, Japan bombed Pearl Harbor, a U.S. Navy base in Hawaii. This surprise attack drew the United States into the war more directly, and many men **enlisted** in the armed forces. Workers were still needed in the factories, so women entered the workforce for the first time, doing the jobs previously for men only.

Some of the country's main military bases were in California. Because California was the Pacific border of the United States, it had to be prepared for enemy strikes. Also, the state's climate and geography made it ideal for training. Soldiers could train in desert, mountainous, and snowy conditions. California training camps included **Fort** Ord, Camp Pendleton, McClellan Air Force Base, and the Treasure Island Naval Base. Thousands of people came to live and train on these bases.

The need for more airplanes during World War II provided jobs for many people in California. Many planes were built by men and women in Long Beach, California.

During World War II, the U.S. government made many Japanese Americans stay in holding camps. This one was near Mount Whitney in California.

JAPANESE AMERICANS

One group in California—people with a Japanese background—faced particularly difficult times during the war. Most were U.S. citizens, yet the U.S. government thought they might send information to **Allied** enemies in Japan. Over 110,000 Japanese Americans from the West Coast were moved to **internment** camps. These families spent three years in shacks surrounded by barbed wire. In 1948, President Harry S Truman signed the Japanese American Evacuation Claims Act, to repay Japanese Americans for what they lost due to their forced evacuation. Unfortunately, this act was not well enforced, and many Japanese Americans never received any money for their suffering.

The 442nd Regiment

Although their families had been sent to camps, some young Japanese-American men joined the army. They formed a unit made up entirely of Japanese Americans. The 442nd Regimental Combat Team took part in the invasion of Italy. It won more medals for bravery than any combat team in U.S. history.

Living in the Modern World

By the time World War II ended in 1945, California was the center of the defense **industry.** All products of the defense industry—planes, ships, bombs, rockets, and missiles—are manufactured in California.

Even though the war was over, the U.S. government continued to purchase planes for the nation's defense. The United States was locked in a new struggle, called the **Cold War,** with the Soviet Union. Although the U.S. and the Soviet Union were not fighting in combat, both governments were developing weapons.

*A U.S. laboratory for developing **nuclear** weapons was opened in Livermore, California, in September 1951. The first U.S. hydrogen bomb test, called "Operation Ivy," took place on November 1, 1952.*

RISING POPULATION

Most people who had moved to California during World War II

stayed. New people came, too, from other states and even other countries, especially Mexico. California cities kept growing. **Suburbs** spread quickly, too, replacing farmland. Whole towns called "developments" popped up almost overnight. Freeways were continuously built to tie these towns together, and the number of cars increased dramatically. Big cities such as Los Angeles began to face the problem of air pollution.

After World War II, suburbs grew quickly around the larger California cities, such as Los Angeles.

EDUCATION

After World War II, many of the jobs in California required special skills. California developed a great system of public colleges to train people to fill those jobs.

The University of California (UC) was founded in 1868. It started with a **campus** in Berkeley. The UC system has plans to open its tenth campus—in Merced—sometime in 2004. A second system, the "state universities," added schools as well. Junior colleges were created, offering specialized technical programs that only required two years of schooling to complete. California currently has more than 80 junior colleges—more than any other state.

Until 1966, students attending public universities in California did not have to pay tuition. However, when Ronald Reagan was elected governor of California in 1966, he cut the funding for the University of California. He then helped create the first set of tuition fees to be paid by students attending the universities.

Other costs became higher in California as well. Politicians were voting to raise property taxes. Many California families were forced to sell their homes. In 1978, Proposition 13 asked for a change in the state constitution that would limit property taxes. People in California were being forced to sell their homes because they could not afford to pay the high taxes on them. The proposition was overwhelmingly approved by voters in California. Soon after, people in other states became interested in the idea of a "tax **revolt.**" Ronald Reagan became the president of the United States in 1980, and he continued the trend of tax cuts for all Americans during his presidency.

Nancy Reagan looks on as her husband, Ronald Reagan, is sworn into office as president of the United States, for the second time, on January 21, 1985.

REFOCUSING THE INDUSTRIES (1989–PRESENT)

The republics of the Soviet Union gained their freedom in 1989. With the **Cold War** at an end, U.S. defense spending went down. Many California military bases had to close. **Aerospace** companies in California lost money and cut almost 150,000 jobs. Today, improving economies in the U.S. and around the world have brought increased spending on aircraft and space vehicles. California is home to about 710 manufacturers of aircraft and parts, 270 makers of search and **navigation** equipment, and 96 producers of spacecraft and parts.

Computer manufacturing is one of the most important **industries** in California. In the mid–1970s, two engineers, Steve Jobs and Steve Wozniak, invented the personal computer. With their new invention, Jobs and Wozniak started a company called Apple. Dozens of other companies sprang up near them. The area between San Francisco and San Jose became known as Silicon Valley, named after one of the materials used in computers. Many of the biggest companies in the computer **industry,** such as

Steve Jobs, shown here in 1979, shows off the chess game program on an Apple II computer—the machine with which he and Steve Wozniak launched their business.

Apple, Microsoft, IBM, Hewlett Packard, Yahoo!, Netscape, and Intel all have offices in Silicon Valley. In 2001, over half the goods exported from California were computers and electronics.

California is also the nation's leader in agricultural exports. Farmers ship more than $6.5 billion in food and other agricultural products around the world each year. Milk and cream, grapes, lettuce, cattle, and hay are some of the top products produced and sold.

Because California is the top agricultural state in the nation, it is also the largest food processing state. California ships over $50 billion worth of food products each year. Food processed in the state includes fruits and vegetables, baked goods, meats, dairy products, sugar, beverages, and fats and oils. Almost 200,000 people work in California's food processing industry.

California is the fourth largest oil-producing state in the United States. During 2001, California's crude-oil production totaled about 293.7 million barrels of oil, or about 800,000 barrels a day. However, the state uses about twice that much oil every day. Around 48,507 oil and gas wells in 28 counties are currently producing in California.

Entertainment technology is a growing industry that continues to thrill moviegoers. California has combined its

California's location on the Pacific coast makes it the ideal place from which to ship goods. California exports goods to over 220 markets worldwide. Over 1.15 million people work in the exporting industry.

entertainment and technology backgrounds to create high-tech products. Animation, special effects, video games, and computer programming are all products of entertainment technology. California has over half of all motion picture production jobs found in the United States, making it the industry leader.

ALWAYS CHANGING

California's rich history, varied landscape, natural resources, and the diversity of its people have shaped it into the place it is today. California's residents have seen the state through both prosperous and tough times, and the ideas and innovations of future generations will continue to transform the state.

California's oil refineries are located in the San Francisco Bay area, Los Angeles area, and the Central Valley.

Map of California

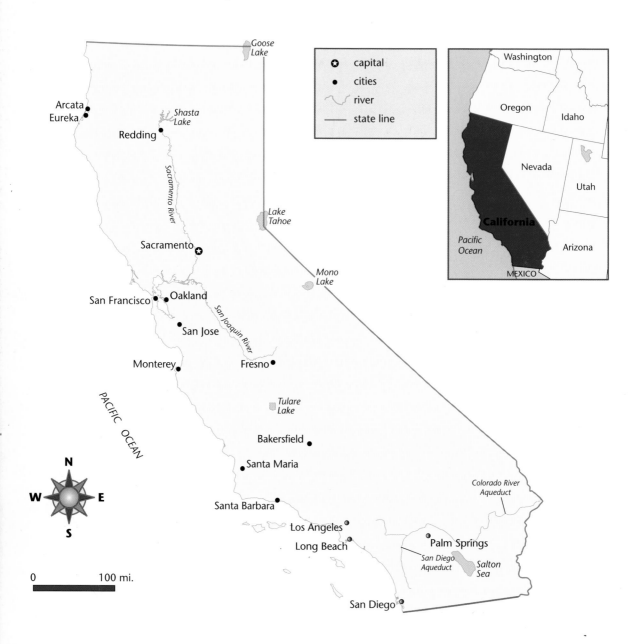

capital
cities
river
state line

Goose Lake
Arcata
Eureka
Redding
Shasta Lake
Sacramento River
Sacramento
San Francisco
Oakland
San Jose
Monterey
Lake Tahoe
Mono Lake
San Joaquin River
Fresno
Tulare Lake
Bakersfield
Santa Maria
Santa Barbara
Los Angeles
Long Beach
San Diego
Palm Springs
Colorado River Aqueduct
San Diego Aqueduct
Salton Sea

PACIFIC OCEAN

N
W E
S

0   100 mi.

Washington
Oregon
Idaho
Nevada
Utah
California
Pacific Ocean
Arizona
MEXICO

Timeline

1512	Hernán Cortés reaches the North American continent
1542	Juan Rodríguez Cabrillo reaches San Diego Bay
1579	Sir Francis Drake visits California
1769	Father Junipero Serra founds **Mission** San Diego
1821	Spanish rule ends in Mexico
1826	Jedediah Smith enters California from the east
1834	Mission lands are given to private families
1846	Bear Flag **Revolt** takes place
1848	The United States gains California
1848	Gold is discovered at Sutter's Mill
1850	California becomes a state
1858	Overland Mail Service started
1862	The "Big Four" found the Central Pacific Railroad Company
1868	University of California is founded
1869	**Transcontinental** railroad is completed
1882	The Chinese Exclusion Act is passed
1887	Los Angeles real estate boom reaches its height
1906	San Francisco earthquake occurs
1908	First movie studio begins in Los Angeles
1913	Los Angeles **aqueduct** is completed
1915	Panama Canal is completed
1933	First mass-produced commercial aircraft is created in Santa Monica
1939	Law passed to prevent "Dust Bowl" residents from moving to California
1951	Lawrence Livermore Laboratory opens
1962	California becomes the state with the most people
1966	Ronald Reagan is elected governor
1976	Apple Computer is started
1978	Proposition 13 passes
1998	California celebrates 150 years since the gold rush
2000	California celebrates 150th anniversary of its statehood
2002	Collapse of the "dot-coms" in Silicon Valley

Glossary

abolitionist   person who wanted to ban slavery

adobe   heavy clay used to make sun dried bricks

aerospace   having to do with air and space travel

agent   person who acts on behalf of someone

agriculturalist   person who grows crops and raises animals to sell

Allies   nations that sided with France and England in World War II

annexation   adding something to something else in order to become a part of it

annual   every year

aqueduct   structure that carries water a long distance

blacksmithing   making things out of iron by heating and hammering it

campus   grounds of a university or other school

catastrophe   terrible event

Catholic   one who belongs to the Catholic Church, the branch of Christianity centered in Rome

Catholic Church   original church of Christianity centered in Rome, Italy

chaps   leather flaps worn by cowboys over their pants to protect their legs

Christianity   religion based on the life and teachings of Jesus Christ

citrus   fruits including lemons, limes, grapefruits, and oranges

Cold War   competition, tension, and conflict short of actual war between the Soviet Union and the United States

commodore   high ranking naval officer

Congress   lawmaking group of the United States

conquest   process of forcefully taking over land from another group

constitutional convention meeting of delegates to write or change a constitution

culture   ideas, skills, arts, and a way of life of a certain people at a certain time

depression   time when businesses are doing poorly

dust bowl   farming area dried out by lack of rainfall

emigrate   leave a country or region and settle somewhere else

enlisted   joined the armed forces as a volunteer

ethnic   belonging to a group with a particular culture

fort   enclosed area built to withstand attack

graze   roam over a grassland feeding on plants

immigrant   person who moves to one country from another to live

industry/industrial   group of businesses that offer a similar product or service

internment   to be confined during a war

interpreter   person who explains what someone speaking another language is saying

land grant   giving of land by the government to encourage building

mission   small town based around a church

missionary   person sent by a church to spread his or her religious beliefs

navigation   steering or directing the course of

nuclear   powered by the energy released when an atom is split

peninsula   finger of land sticking out into a body of water

pen name   false name an author uses on his or her work

Prohibition Party   political organization that opposes the sale and consumption of alcoholic beverages

province   main division of a country, similar to a state

pueblo   Spanish word meaning "town"

rancho   huge estate; Spanish word meaning "ranch"

revolt   violent uprising against authority

Richter scale   system by which the strength of an earthquake is expressed

riot   sudden outbreak of violence by a crowd

rodeo   contest in which cowboys compete in events based on ranch work

secularize   to remove the religious connection

suburb   one of the small communities surrounding a city

surplus   amount left over

survey   study of land to determine its boundaries and features

tanning   process by which an animal hide is tanned

telegraphic   sending messages by code over connecting wires

transcontinental   extending across a continent

trolley   streetcar that runs on tracks

Union   group of states that formed the federal government during the Civil War

More Books to Read

Chambers, Catherine E. *California Gold Rush*. Memphis, Tenn.: Troll Associates, 1998.

Harder, Dan. *A Child's California*. Portland, Oreg.: WestWinds Press, 2000.

Kennedy, Teresa. *California*. Danbury, Conn.: Children's Press, 2001.

Pelta, Kathy. *California*. Minneapolis, Minn.: Lerner Publications, 2001.

Schanzer, Rosalyn, ed. *Gold Fever! Tales from the California Gold Rush*. New York: National Geographic Society, 1999.

Index

442nd Regiment   37

abolitionists   22
agriculture   9–10, 28–29
airplane industry   32, 35–36, 41
air pollution   39
Allies   35, 37
Apple Computer   41–42

Bear Flag Revolt   14, 20
Beckwourth, James   11
Benton, Thomas Hart   12
Bidwell, John   20
Big Four   25, 28
Brannan, Sam   17

Cabrillo, Juan Rodríguez   5
California Republic   14
Californios   10, 11, 15
Catholic Church   7, 10
Chinese Exclusion Act   27
Chinese workers   25, 27
Civil War   24, 26
Clappe, Louise "Dame Shirley"
   17
Clay, Henry   22
Cold War   38, 41
Colorado River   4
Compromise of 1850   22
computer industry   41–43
Comstock Lode   21
Cortés, Hernán   5

defense industry   38
Drake, Sir Francis   5–6
dust-bowl states   34–35

education   39–40
entertainment industry   33,
   42–43

food processing   42
Foreign Miners Tax   19
forty-niners   18
Frémont, John C.   12, 14, 20
Fugitive Slave Act   22

gold rush   17–19, 21, 22
Great Depression   34–35
Guadalupe-Hildago treaty   15

Hollywood   33, 34
Huntington, Collis   25, 29
Huntington, Henry   27

Japanese American Evacuation
   Claims Act   37
Japanese internment   37
Jobs, Steve   41
Judah, Theodore   25

Kearney, Denis   27
Kearny, Stephen   15

Los Angeles   10, 15, 29, 30,
   33, 39, 43

Mexican-American War   12–15,
   16, 20
Mexican government   10–11,
   12–13, 14–15, 16
military bases   35, 36
missions   6–9, 10–11

Native Americans   4–5, 6,
   7–9, 10, 11
New Helvetia   16–17

oil production   42
Operation Ivy   38
Overland mail service   26, 28
Owens Valley–Los Angeles
   Aqueduct   30

Panama Canal   31–32
Panama-Pacific International
   Exposition   32
Pearl Harbor   35
Polk, James   12
Pony Express   27, 28
Portola, Gaspar de   6
presidios   9–10
Proposition 13   40
pueblos   9–10

railroads   25–28
ranchos   9, 11
Reagan, Ronald   40

Sacramento   20, 21, 23, 26
San Francisco   9, 21, 25, 27, 29,
   30–32, 35, 41, 43
San Francisco earthquake
   of 1906   30–31
San Jose   10, 23, 41
San Pascual, Battle of   15
Serra, Junípero   7, 8
ship building   35
Sierra Nevada Mountains   16,
   23, 25, 30
Silicon Valley   42
silver mining   20–21
slavery   22
Slidell, John   12
Sloat, John   14
Smith, Jedediah   11
Spanish explorers   5–7
statehood   22–23
Stockton, Robert   14–15, 20
Sutter, Johann Augustus   16
Sutter's Fort   16–17, 20

transcontinental railroad
   25–27, 28
trolleys   29
Truman, Harry S   37

Ulloa, Francisco de   5
Union   22
University of California system
   39–40

Vallejo, Mariano   10, 14
vaqueros   9

Western Union Telegraph service
   26
women in workforce   36
World War I   32
World War II   35–37, 38
Wozniak, Steve   41

About the Author

Tamim Ansary lives in San Francisco, California. He has worked for twenty years as a textbook editor and writer. His nonfiction series for children include *Holiday Histories* and *Native Americans.* Currently, he writes a learning column for Encarta Online.